Steam in Devon

Peter W. Gray

First published 1995

ISBN 0 7110 2391 3

© Peter W. Gray 1995

IAN ALLAN *Publishing*

Published by Ian Allan Publishing

An imprint of Ian Allan Ltd, Terminal House, Station Approach, Shepperton, Surrey TW17 8AS; printed by Ian Allan Printing Ltd., Coombelands House, Addlestone, Surrey KT15 1HY.

Front cover:
On the steepest part of the climb from Aller Junction to Dainton tunnel, 'Castle' class 4-6-0 No 5053 *Earl Cairns* is making a confident ascent on the short stretch of 1 in 36 with the 6.10pm from Goodrington Sands Halt to Plymouth on 21 July 1960. This was a 'dated' service, which, in 1960, ran from 11 July to 26 August and normally reversed in Platform 8 at Newton Abbot.

Right:
The county boundary between Somerset and Devon runs along the Blackdown Hills, which the railway cuts through in Whiteball tunnel, the construction of which by the Bristol & Exeter Railway delayed the coming of the first through train from London to Exeter by two years. With the tail of the train just clearing the summit close to Whiteball Siding signalbox, 4-6-0 No 5043 *Earl of Mount Edgcumbe* speeds past the Burlescombe distant signal with the 1.20pm (SO) from Paddington to Kingswear on 1 July 1961. The concrete post supporting the signals for the down relief line probably dates from 1927, when this line was installed.

All uncredited photographs were taken by the author.

Introduction

Welcome to Devon — my home county, and one which I am sure most readers will have visited at one time or another.

For those who remember the days of bucket and spade holidays, preceded by a long train journey to the southwest, this will be a nostalgic reminder of those more relaxed times when on summer Saturdays the crowded holiday trains followed each other down the main line every few minutes, while on the many branch lines little trains pottered to and fro serving both the local passengers and the holidaymakers.

For those too young to remember those days, this will exemplify the railway when it was a public service, rather than a profit centre, old fashioned but reliable; a railway where a missed connection was far more likely to result in the running of an extra train, rather than a taxi; a railway which made every endeavour to get you to your destination on rail not road.

This railway then carried much of the nation's freight traffic, though in diminishing quantities, which was soon to lead to the railway's role being re-examined, and with its 'common carrier' status removed, able to refuse traffic deemed 'unprofitable'. This, and vastly increased car ownership during the 1960s, soon led to the almost complete abandonment of the network of Devon branch lines, which had until then acted as feeders to the Southern and Western Region main lines.

One felt at the time that more could have been done to save some of them. The attractions of individual lines could have been promoted, and more economical methods of working adopted; but no, the Western Region management continued to pick off the branch lines one by one for closure and once the Southern Region lines fell into their hands in 1963, these too succumbed.

Today, of the original branch lines in Devon, only those to Exmouth, Barnstaple (Junction) and Paignton remain open in the hands of Regional Railways, while the Southern main line effectively terminates at Exeter St David's, but still exists as a private siding from Crediton to Meldon Quarry. Between St Budeaux (Victoria Rd) and Bere Alston it is used by the Regional Railways trains to Gunnislake, across the Tamar. The Paignton & Dartmouth Steam Railway operate the remainder of the old Kingswear branch beyond Paignton, while the South Devon Railway Trust operates most of the old Ashburton branch between Buckfastleigh and Totnes (Littlehempston). The Plym Valley Railway also hopes soon to be running a short distance from its new terminus above Marsh Mills on the Launceston branch.

For walkers and cyclists, the Tarka Trail uses the trackbed of the Torrington branch and extends along part of the line towards Halwill Junction, passing the preserved signalbox at Instow and Bideford station, where some track has been relaid, along the way.

As you may imagine, compressing the whole of Devon's railways as they existed in the 1957 to 1965 period, into a series of 80 odd pictures has been very difficult, and of the lines open then, one or two are hinted at, rather than illustrated. However, I have endeavoured to present as balanced a portrait as possible of 'Steam in Devon', and will leave the reader to judge.

Those interested in the photographic details may like to know that my early pictures up to the spring of 1959 were taken with a folding Voigtlander Vito IIa 35mm camera which had a f3.5 Color-Skopar lens. Subsequent pictures were taken using an Agfa Super Silette with a superb f2 Solagon fixed lens. Most of the exposures were made on Kodachrome film, the very slow Mark I until early 1962 and Mark II thereafter, with a few Agfa CT18 during the winter months until 1959.

Lastly, I should like to thank those friends who have assisted me with this project, particularly Trevor Owen for the use of a number of 1958 Kodachromes. Also Derek Frost, Alistair Jeffery and Eric Youldon who helped with additional caption material.

Now let us commence our tour of Devon as it was towards the end of the steam era. We shall start at Whiteball tunnel, where the GWR main line entered the county and continue through to Plymouth, taking in some of the branch lines along the way, before travelling north on the Launceston branch, with a sideways glance at Bere Alston. With Launceston itself in Cornwall, we now pick up the Southern line at Halwill Junction and follow this line back through Exeter to Axminster (near the Dorset border), before returning via the East Devon branches to Exeter and then taking the North Devon Line to Torrington and Ilfracombe. The return from North Devon is via the GWR's Barnstaple branch to Morebath Junction, thence over the Exe and Teign Valley lines with a last look at the Kingswear branch, to finish back at Newton Abbot.

Peter W. Gray
Torquay
July 1995

Right: When the London & South Western Railway extended the Salisbury & Yeovil Railway from Yeovil Junction on to Exeter, it provided a line with reasonable gradients and long sweeping curves, the latter amply demonstrated here on the Exeter side of Sidmouth Junction, as Bulleid 'Battle of Britain' class 4-6-2 No 34086 *219 Squadron* races towards Exeter with the 1pm from Waterloo to Plymouth and Ilfracombe on 10 August 1963.

Above:

Amid a forest of semaphore signals, although by 1963 only two posts appear to be wooden ones, 4-6-0 No 7010 *Avondale Castle* thunders through Tiverton Junction station on 1 June at the head of the 12.25pm from Paddington to Paignton. While 0-4-2T No 1442 is away to Tiverton with the branch auto coach, sister engine No 1471 occupies the outer face of the up platform, normally used by the Tiverton train, while shunting a long line of meat containers into the factory at the other end of the station. On the right, the Culm Valley line can be seen curving away on a rising gradient to the point where it would have passed under the M5 motorway, had the line not been closed to all traffic shortly before construction of the proposed bridge was to commence.

Right:

The first branch line to be constructed in Devon was the Bristol & Exeter Railway's single broad gauge line, just over 4 ½ miles long, between Tiverton Junction and Tiverton. Completed in June 1848, with structures wide enough for a second track which was never laid, its principal feature was this magnificent aqueduct carrying the Grand Western Canal across the line near the summit. It is rather ironic that as 0-4-2T No 1471 propelled the 12.50pm from Tiverton Junction on 24 March 1962, the canal above was in a neglected and derelict state. Today the canal has been restored as a Country Park, and the aqueduct remains, but the railway trackbed has largely been returned to farmland.

Culmstock station was typical of those along the branch line to Hemyock. The low winter sunshine warms the red brick station building, similar to those at Uffculme and Hemyock. Supported by local people and constructed under the Culm Valley Light Railway Act of 1873, construction delays put the cost beyond the possibility of operating the line at a profit, and it was eventually sold to the GWR in 1880 for only around half the sum it had cost to build. It was these same local people, however, who later established the successful pioneer butter factory at Hemyock, which in later years was to provide the principal traffic for the branch and sustained it through the 1930s, when many other similar rural branch lines closed. Consequently, it was still possible on 2 December 1961 to see 0-4-2T No 1451 taking the 1.45pm from Tiverton Junction out of Culmstock towards Hemyock, a scene little changed in 80 years. The return journey will be more profitable for the railway, with five or six loaded milk tanks ahead of the old gaslit Barry Railway coach.

The daily pick-up goods was still a feature of the railway scene in 1961, as 2-6-2T No 5560 propels some empty wagons into the up refuge siding at Silverton on 9 December. A shunter awaits the return of the loaded wagons to the yard on the down side, from which a long private siding then extended to the Silverton Paper Mill. Over the years, the several paper mills along the Culm valley provided much traffic for the railway. With its platforms staggered on either side of a road bridge, Silverton, unlike most stations between Taunton and Exeter, retained its original layout to the end.

Above:
At 5.8pm, towards the end of a very busy and unusual day at Exeter St David's station, 4-6-0 No 4999 *Gopsal Hall* takes the 7.30am from Newcastle to Paignton down the through road, next stop Dawlish, where it is due at 5.20pm. The crowd of enthusiasts at the south end of platforms No 3 and 4 take due note, oblivious of the porter trying to restrain a loaded barrow from running away down the platform slope behind them. Why had this day been unusual? Because on 26 August 1961, three up and two down Western Region trains between Paddington and Cornwall had been diverted over the Southern Region between Basingstoke and Plymouth, because of a landslip between Patney & Churton and Westbury.

Right:
October 1960 was a traumatic time for the residents of the lower lying parts of Exeter. Rain had been falling for weeks, and the areas drained by the rivers Creedy, Culm and Exe could take no more. The Exe overflowed its banks filling the Alphington area and the flood plains below with water, partially dammed by the presence of the Exeter by-pass road (A38) across the valley at Countess Wear. It is here that 4-6-0 No 5992 *Horton Hall* is seen running 'light engine' towards its base at Taunton on 22 October 1960.

Above:
In one train the holidaymakers say goodbye to the seaside for another year, while in another excitement mounts as the passengers come in sight of the sea for the first time since leaving London. With a backdrop of Langstone Rock and the English Channel, two 'Castle' class 4-6-0s cross just to the south of Dawlish Warren station; on the left No 5043 *Earl of Mount Edgcumbe* with the 11.40am from Paddington to Penzance heading westward, as Stafford Road based No 5046 *Earl Cawdor* heads for home with the 3.5pm from Paignton to Wolverhampton (Low Level) on Saturday 29 July 1961.

Right:
The pride of the old Great Western Railway was never better expressed than when the 'King' class were introduced in 1927. Thirty-one years later, the 'Kings' were still in front line service as No 6004 *King George III* heads the 7.30am Paddington to Paignton along the sea wall near Dawlish on 16 June 1958.   *T. B. Owen*

Left:
Ever since the South Devon Railway decided to
establish its locomotive factory at Newton Abbot, the
town had been the locomotive headquarters of the south
west, with the GWR Divisional Locomotive
Superintendent's office on the first floor of the new
station building. Situated at the divide between the
easier grades to the east and the severe gradients and
curvature to the west, it was the natural place at which
to change engines in the days of the single-wheelers
and in later years to attach or detach assistant engines.
On summer Saturdays in the 1950s it also became an
engine changing point for many trains proceeding down
the branch to Paignton. This was necessary to save on
'light engine' running, before the new turntable at
Goodrington came into use in 1956, though the
timetable rarely allowed sufficient time for this
operation to be carried out. This scene is typical of
Newton Abbot on a summer Saturday at the end of the
decade, with the new turntable at Goodrington now in
use. It is 6.49am on 29 July 1961 as 4-6-0s No 5946
Marwell Hall and No 6842 *Nunhold Grange* restart the
10.15pm (Friday) from Sheffield, not towards
Plymouth as the double-header might suggest, but
down to Paignton. Standing in platform No 2, and after
a long wait acquiring 2-6-2T No 4103 as a pilot engine,
is 4-6-0 No 1024 *County of Pembroke* on the 8.15pm
(Friday) relief from Keighley to Paignton, which was
the 44th westward train movement since midnight, all
but six of which were loaded passenger trains.

Right:
Under entirely different circumstances, on
22 December 1962, by which time steam on the main
line was much less common, 4-6-0 No 7901 *Dodington
Hall* lifts a pre-Christmas parcels train out of Newton
Abbot on the down main line, with West signalbox
visible above the second van, and the old bow-string
girder road bridge ahead.

Left:
On the bright spring morning of 13 April 1957, west of Newton Abbot, 4-6-0s No 5024 *Carew Castle* and No 1006 *County of Cornwall* move the 12.25am from Manchester (London Road) to Penzance, also conveying through coaches from Glasgow (St Enoch), towards Aller Junction and the foothills of Dartmoor.

Above:
This picture was taken at Langford's bridge, near Aller Junction, at 7pm on 23 July 1959 as 4-6-0 No 7006 *Lydford Castle* hastens the 6.10pm from Goodrington Sands Halt towards Plymouth.
  In the background, 4-6-0 No 5055 *Earl of Eldon* (hidden by some trees) is taking 'The Devonian' express to Paignton, while BR Standard '9F' 2-10-0 No 92225 stands in the loop on a down goods complete with large Prairie banker at the rear.

Left:
On 14 June 1958, 4-6-0s No 5055 *Earl of Eldon* and No 6870 *Bodicote Grange*, with the 1.45pm from Bristol to Newquay and Falmouth, pass Stoneycombe Quarry before entering the 'S' bend below the steep climb to the summit at Dainton tunnel. They had earlier that day piloted up Newquay trains from Plymouth to Newton Abbot. *Trevor B. Owen*

Above:
Churchward designed 2-8-0 No 2809, still in fine voice after 54 years' main line service, approaches the mouth of Dainton tunnel on 3 October 1959 with a Class 'E' express goods, probably the 2.25am Bristol to Tavistock Junction. Rear end assistance from Aller Junction to the tunnel is given by 2-6-2T No 4178.

Left:

At the western end of Dainton tunnel, the Ashburton goods restarts down the steep twisting gradient towards Totnes, after pausing at the Stop Board to pin down brakes. Because of the gable summit at Dainton — a relic of Brunel's original intention to work the line atmospherically, with a pumping house at Dainton — there were two stop boards, one on either side of the signalbox, for short or long goods trains. Until its withdrawal in 1955, 2-6-2T No 4405 had been the regular Ashburton goods engine, succeeded now by light weight 0-6-0PT No 1608, which on 6 August 1959 had been banked to the tunnel by 2-6-2T No 5196. The loaded coal wagons are probably bound for Totnes and the cattle vans for next week's Buckfastleigh market.

Above:

The last Wednesday in June was Buckfastleigh Combined Sunday Schools' Excursion Day, normally an outing to Teignmouth, which took place for four years after the branch officially closed to passengers.

On 28 June 1961 4-6-0 No 4975 *Umberslade Hall* brings the return excursion back into Totnes (during the day the empty stock had been stabled at Exminster) where the train will reverse in the down platform, before being hauled back to Buckfastleigh by 2-6-2Ts Nos 4555 and 4561. These engines can be seen beyond the goods shed. After returning the empty stock to Totnes, the two tank engines went their separate ways, No 4555 to Newton Abbot and No 4561 to Laira.

Above:

The arrival at Ashburton of the official last British Railways train, a Plymouth Railway Circle sponsored brake van special on 8 September 1962, is a time for mixed feelings for those taking part. A brief glimpse of the sun illuminates 2-6-2T No 4567 as it prepares to run around the train, watched by a few locals who have turned out for the occasion, and the participants in the railtour, some of whom will be prominent in the affairs of the Dart Valley Railway Association, soon to be providing volunteer labour for the infant Dart Valley Railway.

Right:

In the final spring of the normal passenger service on the Ashburton branch, Collett 0-4-2T No 1470 hurries along the east bank of the River Dart with the 4.55pm from Totnes on 3 May 1958. Only a short distance beyond the 'Royal Mile', where the Royal Train was sometimes stabled overnight with an attendant 'Castle' class 4-6-0, one passenger stands to admire the view, not far from the pool where students from the nearby Dartington School were wont to go 'skinny dipping' on occasions.

Left:
Following the very wet spell in October 1960 — perhaps some early 'leaves on the line' were experienced — considerable trimming was done in this cutting on the steepest part of Rattery bank, about half a mile below Tigley signalbox. This enabled a clear view to be obtained of 4-6-0 No 6938 *Corndean Hall* racing down the bank towards Totnes with the 12.20pm Penzance to Kensington milk train on 18 August 1961.

Above:
Not all express engines were kept spotlessly clean and evidently 4-6-0 No 5085 *Evesham Abbey*, one of the 1939 conversions from the final 1922 batch of 'Stars', was not Bristol Bath Road's favourite engine! Nevertheless, it is only eight minutes late, steaming through Brent station with the 'Cornishman', the 9am from Wolverhampton to Penzance, on 26 March 1960, when Brent was still for a few more years the junction station for the Kingsbridge branch.

Above:
There were only three intermediate stations on the Kingsbridge branch — Avonwick, Gara Bridge and Loddiswell — of which only Gara Bridge was a crossing station. Here, on 16 June 1958, No 5558 is running in on the 4.15pm from Kingsbridge while No 5533 waits with the 4.15pm from Brent. *Trevor B. Owen*

Above right:
On 3 June 1961 it is only a few days before the end of regular daily steam workings on the Kingsbridge branch as 2-6-2T No 5573 stands at the head of the 12.20pm departure to Brent. Several of the branch workings in this timetable were designated as 'mixed', but not this one. Nevertheless there is a brake van attached behind the single passenger coach. Beyond the well filled goods yard a Western National double-decker waits to connect with the next train.

Below right:
The next train was the 12.24pm from Brent, due into Kingsbridge at 12.58pm and headed by 2-6-2T No 4561. Immediately after arrival No 4561 detached from the train and ran around it, stopping at the water column to replenish the tanks, before picking up the stock and putting it away in the black carriage shed seen in the top picture.

WAY OUT

IVYBRIDGE

Left:
At 5.10pm on Saturday 24 August 1957, the fireman takes a last look back to see that all is well, as the driver opens up the regulator on 2-6-0 No 5356, taking the 4.32pm from Plymouth out of Ivybridge, an 'all stations' service to Exeter. Even on summer Saturdays in 1957, there were five up and four down stopping trains serving the seven stations between Plymouth and Newton Abbot. The original station building stands well back from the trains because the replacement double track viaduct was built to the south of the original Brunel timber structure.

Above:
Trains leaving Plymouth in the up direction face a gruelling two mile climb at 1 in 42 up Hemerdon bank. On Saturday 14 June 1958 4-6-0s No 6849 *Walton Grange* and No 5065 *Newport Castle* are nearing the top of the climb with the 8.20am from Penzance to Paddington. *Trevor B. Owen*

Above left:
On 6 February 1960, in the final days of semaphore signals at Plymouth station — the previous suffix North Road was dropped on the closure of Friary station in 1958 — 0-6-0PT No 6400 takes the 10.20am Saturdays only 'sandwich' auto out past North Road West signalbox. This Saturday only working, 21 miles out to Doublebois, was the longest trip normally undertaken by the Plymouth auto trains. Here it had a long layover before returning at 12.30pm, to arrive back into Plymouth in good time for passengers to visit the Argyle football ground or city centre shops.

Below left: Two months later, on 16 April 1960, the same train is seen entering Devon on its return journey from Doublebois, this time in charge of 0-6-0PT No 6419. In the background work is proceeding on the new road bridge across the River Tamar, the crane on top of the Devon pier having recently pierced the skyline. Soon Brunel's masterpiece, the Royal Albert Bridge, will no longer alone dominate the landscape. Single line working over the bridge then demanded the possession of a token by the driver of each train.

Above:
Plymouth Friary station, the Southern Region terminus, was somewhat inconveniently built facing east, since the trains to Exeter and Waterloo had first to turn through 180 degrees to gain the Western main line at Lipson Junction, before travelling westwards through North Road station. On 30 September 1961, just over three years after the closure of Friary station to passengers, a Plymouth Railway Circle special is making a final journey out to Turnchapel and back behind ex-LSWR Class 'M7' 0-4-4T No 30034.

On 16 August 1959 4-6-0s No 7916 *Mobberley Hall* and No 5061 *Earl of Birkenhead* lead the 10.30am (Sunday) Penzance to Wolverhampton out of Plymouth past Laira Junction signalbox. In the foreground is the boarded way of the 4ft. 6in. gauge Lee Moor Tramway, which although long out of regular commercial use, still maintained its right of way with the annual passage of a horse and wagon, controlled by signals on either side of the main line. As it is a Sunday there are several auto sets in the carriage sidings on the up side, while in the background is the Laira locomotive depot. This was first established on the site in 1901, when a large roundhouse was constructed. It was extended in 1931 when a straight shed was built alongside and continued in use until replaced by the new diesel depot in 1964.

Trevor B. Owen

Another use for the Plymouth auto sets was on the short workings over the Launceston branch, out as far as Tavistock South. This train is the 2.10pm from Plymouth to Tavistock, leaving Marsh Mills behind 0-6-0PT No 6430 on the penultimate Saturday of passenger services over the branch on 22 December 1962. The smoking chimney of the Marsh Mills signal-box can be seen in the far right background. The track leading away from the branch, in the foreground, is dropping sharply down to the Coypool Military Depot, on the lower edge of the site occupied by the Plym Valley Preservation Society, whose members have already relaid some of the branch track and hope one day soon to operate trains in the direction of Bickleigh.

Left:
The principal station on the Southern route out of Plymouth between Devonport (King's Road) and Tavistock North was Bere Alston, junction for the Callington branch. At Bere Alston on Saturday 1 April 1961, Ivatt Class 2 2-6-2T No 41317 has just retrieved from the up main line two through coaches for Callington, left by the Saturdays only 12.23pm Plymouth to Tavistock North. This train, appropriately worked by 'West Country' class 4-6-2 No 34011 *Tavistock*, can be seen in the far distance, under a trail of steam. The Callington service will leave Bere Alston at 1pm.

Above:
Between Tavistock and Lydford the Southern main line and the much earlier GWR branch to Launceston follow the same valley, with the Southern line crossing over the Launceston branch at this point, about one mile south of Mary Tavy and Blackdown station (see next page) on the Launceston branch. On the Southern line an unidentified class 'M7' 0-4-4T hurries along between stops at Brentor and Tavistock North.

Trevor B. Owen

Above:
Probably qualifying at the time for the title 'Most closed looking station still open in Devon', Mary Tavy and Blackdown, seen here from the 10.40am Plymouth to Launceston on 22 December 1962, had then been unstaffed for over 20 years. However, as the abandoned signalbox indicates, it had seen much busier times between 1876 and 1890, when the LSWR trains were using this part of the GWR's Launceston branch to gain access to their terminus at Devonport, via Marsh Mills. The passing loop and signalbox were taken out of use in 1892 and 70 years later all the glass appears to be intact. Were we just imagining the more peaceful times of yesteryear ?

Right:
Another picturesque station on the top section of the Launceston branch was Coryton, with 2-6-2T No 4570 on the 3.5pm from Plymouth on 4 August 1962. The lighter shade of rust on the siding leading in from the running line shows that some use has been made of it recently, but the cattle pens have long since despatched their last animal.

Above:
The original Halwill & Beaworthy became Halwill Junction when the North Cornwall line opened to Launceston in 1886. Previously the only line here had been the one going to Holsworthy, later extended to Bude by the LSWR. It is on this line that BR Standard Class '4' 2-6-4T No 80039 stands with the coaches it had earlier brought in as the 9.30am from Bude and will shortly attach to the rear of the train now running in. This is the 8.30am from Padstow to Waterloo, hauled by Maunsell 'N' class 2-6-0 No 31846, still with some vestige of its lined black livery, where some kind soul has cleaned the cabside. The nearside track is that of the North Devon & Cornwall Junction Light Railway, completed by the SR in 1925, on which Ivatt 2-6-2T No 41283 has run in with the 8.52am from Torrington on 22 August 1964.

Left:
This picture was taken from almost the same spot a few minutes later, but now looking south. The Torrington train is in the foreground, but as it pulls away after attaching the Bude coach, No 80039's exhaust hides the goods yard located to the left of the Halwill Junction abattoir. 2-6-4T No 80041 rests in the down Bude bay platform.

Left:
Without doubt Meldon viaduct is the most impressive structure on any of the Southern Railway lines in Devon. Standing some 120ft above the sparkling West Okement river, its six steel spans take the line across the valley on a 30 chain radius curve. It is structurally interesting because when originally built the line was single. When the second track was added in 1879, another almost identical viaduct was built alongside the first, with the legs of the centre piers intertwined. With the main line to Plymouth approaching its summit of 950ft above sea level, the viaduct gave passengers superb views, both to the north across the rolling hills towards Hatherleigh and south to the highest tors of Dartmoor. Crossing Meldon viaduct at the regulation 20mph with the up Plymouth to Brighton service on 19 July 1958 is unrebuilt 'West Country' class Pacific No 34023 *Blackmore Vale*.

Trevor B. Owen

Right:
The line reached Okehampton in 1871, constructed by the Devon & Cornwall Railway but was soon absorbed into the LSWR. On 4 August 1964, only a month before the end of the traditional service operated by the Southern Region, we see from the platform the departure of a short goods train, mainly consisting of heavy loaded ballast hoppers, behind Ivatt 2-6-2T No 41317 and 'N' class 2-6-0 No 31406. Outside the engine shed, a sub-shed of Exmouth Junction, is BR Standard 2-6-4T No 80059, already wearing the Bude disc headcode, which will later work the 3.35pm service from Okehampton to Bude. Also on shed was BR Standard 4-6-0 No 75022, but as this was by the turntable it is hidden by the train engines.

Left:
The drab tones of 'N' class 2-6-0 No 31836, as it drifts down from Crediton with the 6am Class 9 Goods from Barnstaple Junction to Exmouth Junction on 23 August 1963, contrast with the multitude of bright summer flowers in the cottage garden alongside. The generous width of the formation here, approaching Newton St Cyres station, can be traced back to the original broad gauge Exeter & Crediton Railway, opened in 1851.

Above:
It was not until 1860 that the LSWR completed its line to what was Exeter Queen Street station, which became Exeter Central on completion of the present station in 1933. On 13 July 1963 the driver of rebuilt 'West Country' class Pacific No 34036 *Westward Ho!* oils round, before backing down onto the front half of the 10.30am to Waterloo, which has just arrived behind unrebuilt Pacific No 34106 *Lydford* as the 8.10am from Ilfracombe.

Meanwhile a restaurant car will have been added to the Ilfracombe portion by one of the bankers, and No 34036 will then pull the combined formation forward until it is clear of the scissors to await the arrival of the 8.25am from Plymouth, when the process will be repeated. Nineteen minutes were allowed for the whole process to be completed, but the keen Southern crews could do it in a lot less than this, when necessary. In the down side bay platform, rebuilt Pacific No 34003 *Plymouth* waits on the 10.37am 'all stations', except St James Park Halt, to Templecombe.

Above left:
Leaving Exeter Central for Waterloo, there is a sharp climb at 1 in 100 through Blackboy tunnel to Exmouth Junction, where the Exmouth branch peels away to the right, while to the left is the Exmouth Junction locomotive depot. Outside the depot, gleaming in the morning sun, is rebuilt Bulleid 'Merchant Navy' class Pacific No 35023 *Holland-Afrika Line*, which came new to Exmouth Junction, but on 3 October 1963 was based at Bournemouth. The Western Region takeover from January 1963 is indicated by the presence of an ex-GWR pannier tank ahead of the Pacific.

Below left:
With clouds lowering over the distant hills, Maunsell 'S15' class 4-6-0 No 30843 waits for permission to enter Sidmouth Junction with the 2.8pm from Axminster to Exeter Central on Saturday 10 August 1963. This train had started from Yeovil Town at 11.52am, but took a long break at Axminster. Passing at speed on the up road is rebuilt 'Battle of Britain' 4-6-2 No 34071 *601 Squadron* with the Padstow and Bude portion of the 'Atlantic Coast Express'.

Above:
On 3 August 1964 with the multi-portioned weekday 'Atlantic Coast Express' trailing on its drawbar, rebuilt 'Merchant Navy' class Pacific No 35028 *Clan Line* approaches the mouth of Honiton tunnel at the summit of the almost five mile climb, mostly at 1 in 90 to 1 in 100.

Above:

A busy scene at Seaton Junction on a very hazy 3 August 1963. In preparation for the arrival of the 'Seaton Buffet Express', the branch train, since the Western Region takeover now 0-6-0PT No 6400 and two auto coaches, has been parked out of the way in the sidings on the down side of the main line. At 1.45pm 'West Country' class Pacific No 34095 *Brentor* arrived with the 'Seaton Buffet Express', which, having already detached the rear coaches at Axminster for Lyme Regis, now had the Buffet portion at the rear. With the passengers still aboard, this Buffet portion

was shunted into the siding alongside the branch platform and detached. The train was then pulled out, to be propelled back once more on to Maunsell 'U' class 2-6-0 No 31792 which was waiting at the far end of the branch platform, tender first, to take it down to Seaton. As the coach at the Seaton end of the train approaches No 31792 at 1.50pm, controlled by the flagman, on the up main line rebuilt 'Battle of Britain' class Pacific No 34062 *17 Squadron* races through on the 11.10am Plymouth to Brighton service.

Right:

In the final year of the traditional service on the Seaton branch, ex-LSWR 'M7' class 0-4-4T No 30048 arrives at Seaton Junction from Seaton on 11 June 1962. The Seaton branch was the last in East Devon to be regularly worked by 'M7' class 0-4-4Ts, which together with the smaller 'O2' class 0-4-4Ts had in earlier years more or less monopolised the East Devon branches, except, of course, for Lyme Regis.

The LSWR's main line entered Devon only about a mile and a half to the east of Axminster, where 'West Country' class 4-6-2 No 34030 *Watersmeet* has recently arrived on the 12.36pm Salisbury to Exeter stopping service. Today, although the signalbox and the elegant barley-sugar columns of the gas lamps have long since disappeared, the station building remains, but with the chimney breasts now reduced in height. With the closure of the Lyme Regis branch in 1965, and the singling of the main line, the up side platforms are now abandoned and the fine glazed footbridge has gone. Nevertheless on 2 November 1963, Ivatt 2-6-2T No 41320 was taking water prior to taking out the 2.40pm service to Lyme Regis.

From the glazed footbridge at Axminster, the view westwards shows that the Lyme Regis branch curved away sharply to the right, before rounding an old wartime pill-box and then swinging back across the main line and away to the south behind the Axminster Carpets factory. The locomotive in this view taken on 22 June 1958 is No 30582, one of the three Adams Radial 4-4-2Ts regularly used on this line until 1960.

The train is half Maunsell corridor, stood down from main line duty and half ex-LSWR non-corridor, still in the early BR red livery.

Trevor B. Owen

Left:
The Lyme Regis branch was characterised by steep gradients and above all by sharp curves, which arose from its construction as the Axminster & Lyme Regis Light Railway, opened in August 1903. Adams Radial 4-4-2T No 30583 is climbing to the summit of the line at Combpyne with a Saturday extra service from Axminster on 18 June 1960. This engine has had a chequered history: built for the LSWR by Neilson & Co. of Glasgow in 1885, it was sold to the Ministry of Munitions in 1917, sold again to the East Kent Railway in 1919, bought back by the Southern Railway in 1946 and is now the only one of the class in preservation.

Above:
The days of spotlessly clean Exmouth Junction engines are well in the past as BR Standard class 4 2-6-4T No 80036 prepares to leave Sidmouth Junction with the 10.55am to Sidmouth on 2 November 1963 and `West Country´ class Pacific No 34024 *Tamar Valley* exits on the 10.30am from Exeter Central to Waterloo.

Tipton St Johns station, seen in the background of this picture, was the junction between the original Sidmouth branch of 1874 and the much later line to Budleigh Salterton opened in 1897, and later extended to Exmouth. At 11.10am on Sunday 15 June 1958, when the engines were being cleaned, ex-LSWR 'M7' class 0-4-4T No 30025 is storming out of Tipton up the 1 in 45 gradient towards Sidmouth. On the way down from Sidmouth Junction this train had crossed with sister engine No 30024, and when the latter had returned and departed for Sidmouth at 11.55am, BR Standard Class '3' 2-6-2T No 82022, which had arrived from Exmouth at 11.5am, will push its train back into the station, eventually leaving for Exmouth at 12 noon.

Trevor B. Owen

Budleigh Salterton was a terminus for just over six years, until the LSWR completed the line through to Exmouth in June 1903. This enabled through trains to be run between Waterloo and Exmouth via the new line and this service continued until 1964. On 15 August that year, when BR first introduced the 24 hour clock, BR Standard Class '3' 2-6-2T No 82042 stands on the 1.34pm Exmouth to Waterloo, waiting for the eight-coach Exmouth portion of the 9am from Waterloo to clear the station behind sister engine No 82035 and BR Standard Class '4' 2-6-4T No 80038.

Above:

Exmouth station on 2 November 1963, only a few days before the start of DMU operation and the closure of the small locomotive depot, the end of which is visible on the right, with Ivatt 2-6-2T No 41316 standing outside. BR Standard 2-6-4T No 80041 has arrived on the 11.15am from Tipton St John's, while BR Standard 2-6-2T No 82001 is preparing to leave on the return service at 11.50am. With two commodious island platforms, Exmouth was well equipped to deal with these trains as well as the frequent direct service from

Exeter and on summer Saturdays, through services to Waterloo, Manchester and, until the demise of the Somerset & Dorset route, to Cleethorpes.

Right:

Two proposals were made for broad gauge railways to Exmouth, both leaving the South Devon Railway line between Countess Wear and Exminster, with bridges across the River Exe and the Exeter Canal. Neither was started before the imminent arrival of the LSWR from

the east convinced shareholders they would be better served with a standard gauge line from Exmouth Junction. On 7 July 1963 as BR Standard 2-6-4T No 80038 was setting forth from Lympstone towards Exeter with the 5.45pm from Exmouth, the fate of the Exmouth branch was seemingly sealed. Dr Beeching had proposed its closure. However, it escaped closure and now has a frequent service to Exeter and Paignton with another new station opened in 1995.

Left:
The LSWR opened its extension down the hill (1 in 37) to St David's in February 1862, and very close to 101 years later, on an extremely cold 26 January 1963, 'Battle of Britain' 4-6-2 No 34086 *219 Squadron* approaches with the 8.41am from Exeter Central to Plymouth. While not much snow is in evidence, the whole country was then in the grip of two months of unrelenting frost. Just off picture to the

right, 0-6-0PT No 3794 was in steam with a rather crude snowplough fitted and beyond, 0-4-2T No 1470 and 2-6-0 No 7311 both stood frozen and forlorn, awaiting their final journey.

Above:
There are several picturesque stations along the North

Devon line between Coleford Junction and Barnstaple Junction, none more so than Lapford, seen here at 1.20pm on Bank Holiday Monday 5 August 1963. Note the unusual layout, with the original single line platform on the left, but the down platform added later is beyond the road bridge but on the same side of the other line.

Above:

Between Barnstaple Junction and Torrington the railway was extended in stages, eventually reaching Torrington in 1872, where this goods yard later became the terminus of the 3ft 0in gauge Torrington & Marland Light Railway, which approached from the west, on a wooden viaduct over the river. The narrow gauge line terminated between the two sidings in the foreground. In 1925 the North Devon & Cornwall Junction Light Railway opened through to Halwill Junction, using the trackbed of the former narrow gauge line, and Torrington then became the terminus of the two branches. In this view, on 21 June 1958, the station is on the left, behind the milk lorry; beyond it, above the goods shed can be seen the roof of the engine shed. An 'M7' class 0-4-4T is moving in the shed yard. On the right, beyond the cattle dock, another 'M7' is leaving on the 4.5pm (SO) semi-fitted goods to Nine Elms, while Ivatt 2-6-2T No 41298 shunts some vans prior to taking out the 4.40pm to Halwill Junction.

Trevor B. Owen

Right:

On 26 August 1963 Ivatt 2-6-2T No 41213 is arriving at Barnstaple Junction with the 4.15pm from Bideford to Nine Elms. The siding behind the train was a wartime extension of the headshunt to the private siding beyond the gate seen above the first container.

Above:

The line from Barnstaple Junction to Ilfracombe was opened in 1874, its principal features being a wrought iron bridge describing a quarter segment of a circle across the River Taw, and the mountainous climb from Braunton up to Mortehoe & Woolacombe station, thence down again to Ilfracombe. It is on the climb from Braunton and nearing the end of the three miles at 1 in 40 that we find 'West Country' class Pacific No 34107 *Blandford Forum*, with Maunsell 'N' class 2-6-0 No 31846 banking, on the Saturday 12.5pm from Waterloo to Ilfracombe. Evidence that the Pacific is working hard can be seen from the little wisps of blue smoke arising from the grass where red-hot cinders have landed.

Right:

Until 1962 ex-LSWR 'M7' class 0-4-4Ts were regularly used as assistant engines over Mortehoe bank. In this view 'M7' No 30667 is piloting ex-GWR 2-6-0 No 7337, as they drift down the gradient towards Ilfracombe with the 8.50am from Taunton on 1 September 1962.

Above:

The precipitous nature of the drop into Ilfracombe and the busy summer Saturday service are both well illustrated in this view taken on 13 July 1963 . With 'N' class 2-6-0 No 31849 and 'West Country' class Pacific No 34011 *Tavistock* barely clear of the station on the 12 noon to Waterloo and over two miles of 1 in 36 ahead of them, already the 7.50am from Yeovil Town is signalled into the platform they have just left. The other platform is occupied by 'N' class 2-6-0 No 31853 and ex-GWR 2-6-0 No 7333 double-heading the 12.25pm to Taunton. The station was perched on a hill over 200ft above the Bristol Channel.

Trevor B. Owen

Right:

The last steam working out of Ilfracombe was 'The Exmoor Ranger', a Railway Correspondence and Travel Society/Plymouth Railway Circle sponsored railtour on 27 March 1965. This ran from Exeter via Okehampton, Halwill Junction, Torrington and Barnstaple Junction to Barnstaple Victoria Road, the original terminus of the GWR branch from Taunton, thence back through Barnstaple Junction to Ilfracombe.

The two Ivatt 2-6-2Ts that had hauled it thus far now becoming bankers, while ex-GWR 2251 class 0-6-0 No 3205, which had banked out of Braunton and followed from Mortehoe down to Ilfracombe, became the train engine. At Filleigh, on the GWR Barnstaple branch, the loop has recently been lifted, as No 3205 steams through with the 'Exmoor Ranger' on its way to Taunton, where it will turn on the shed turntable, before completing the journey back to Exeter.

Trevor B. Owen

Above:

As its name implies, the Devon & Somerset Railway, which became the GWR's Barnstaple branch from Taunton, crossed the county boundary more than once. The principal crossing station at Dulverton was in Somerset, but before reaching Morebath Junction Halt the line was back in Devon again, where, on 13 April 1963, we see ex-GWR 2-6-0 No 6327 on the 4.10pm from Barnstaple standing in the Halt, before resuming its journey to Taunton.

Right:

It was at Morebath Junction that the Exe Valley trains joined the Barnstaple branch. Also on 13 April 1963, after depositing a few passengers at the Halt, the 3.25pm from Exeter St David's pulls away towards Dulverton, where the Exe Valley line trains terminated.

Above:

Icefield Tiverton! Another picture from early 1963, when I had been taking some pictures amid the minor snowdrifts near Halberton Halt, and travelled into Tiverton for some warmth in the steam-heated auto trailer while consuming my sandwiches, before returning for another session. It is 2 February 1963 as 0-4-2T No 1421 waits in the bay platform until 1.20pm, before returning to Tiverton Junction. In the background sister engine No 1450 is propelling the 12.30pm from Dulverton out towards Exeter. Note the row of icicles hanging from No 1421's brake gear and buffer beam.

Right:

On the run down the Exe Valley from Tiverton to Stoke Canon the first crossing place was at Cadeleigh. On Whit Saturday 20 May 1961, 0-4-2T No 1470 is in the background, pulling away towards Tiverton on the 3.20pm from Exeter St David's to Dulverton, while in the foreground, having got the 3.30pm from Bampton on the move out of Cadeleigh, the driver has closed the regulator, to enable the fireman to bring the valve gear back to the running position, before pulling away towards Exeter. Devon County Council had the intention to create a transport museum at Cadeleigh, but this scheme now seems to have fallen through.

Left:

On a glorious 8 June 1963, Thorverton station basks in the evening light. The archetypal country station is almost unchanged by the passage of time since its opening in May 1885. Reminding us of prewar days, when over 75% of the station revenue came from goods traffic, a horsebox stands close by the cattle pens and a line of wagons in the coal yard, next to the 5-ton wooden-jib yard crane. On the siding added in 1898, leading to Thorverton Mill, several empty grain silos wait to be picked up by the next branch goods train. On the river bank there is a Scout camp site, while above and beyond it can be seen the next station — Up Exe Halt. Leading the 5.15pm from Dulverton, propelled by 0-4-2T No 1466, is one of the two named auto trailers 'Thrush', while pulling away towards Tiverton on the 5.48pm from Exeter St David's is 0-6-0PT No 3659.

Above:

The Teign Valley line turned westwards off the main line at City Basin Junction, south of Exeter St Thomas station, to head up into the Haldon hills. With two Collett ex-main line coaches forming the 12.46pm from Exeter St David's through to Newton Abbot via Heathfield, 0-6-0PT No 7761 is pulling away from the stop at Ide on 1 March 1958. *Colour-Rail/P.W. Gray*

On the other side of the Haldon hills, also on 1 March 1958, 2-6-2T No 5536, resplendent in lined green livery, leaves Dunsford Halt, opened in 1928, with the 10.43am from Heathfield to Exeter St David's. Opened by the Exeter Railway in July 1903, this northern section of the Teign Valley line made an end-on junction at Christow with the earlier Teign Valley Railway, which had opened in 1882 and for its first 10 years was an isolated standard gauge line in an otherwise broad gauge area of South Devon.

On 28 February 1959, the last day of passenger services on the Moretonhampstead branch, 0-4-2T No 1466 tackles the gradient above Pullabrook Halt with the heavily loaded 12.50pm from Newton Abbot. Until 1955, Pullabrook Halt had been named Hawkmoor Halt, but it was renamed to avoid confusion with the local Hawkmoor Sanatorium, which to some visitors' dismay they found to be some two miles distant from the Halt, along winding country lanes. The gradient here is at 1 in 53 as the train crosses the River Wrey, on its way to Lustleigh, one of the two original intermediate stations on the line when it was opened by the Moretonhampstead & South Devon Railway in 1866.

On 19 February 1959, 0-4-2T No 1466, the representative of the class later chosen for preservation by the Great Western Society, is standing clear of the timber roofed Moretonhampstead station, with auto trailer No W241W, waiting to propel back to Newton Abbot at 3.15pm. In the background can be seen the broad mouth of an engine shed built for Brunel's 7ft 0¼in gauge. This was in use until 1947, when it would normally have housed a '45XX' class 2-6-2T overnight. The Directors of the M&SDR always harboured the desire to extend their railway to Chagford, and possibly with this in mind both tracks extended a short distance beyond the station building. Behind the camera in this view, where the right hand track was on longitudinal timbers through the cattle dock, there were still one or two South Devon Railway chairs supporting the rail.

On 19 February 1959, standing on what is now the Bovey by-pass road, large Prairie tank No 4150 waits in Bovey station while parcels are loaded into the 10.15am from Moretonhampstead to Newton Abbot. The train is already 15min late, due to additional time taken at the terminus to remove and shunt into the yard a van taken out as tail traffic on the previous train. It is a beautiful, if somewhat misty morning in South Devon, but up country there is thick fog and frost with which to contend.

At Newton Abbot the 5.30am from Paddington is posted as running 77min late that morning, and the next Moretonhampstead departure, behind 0-4-2T No 1466, was held for 10min to ensure connection with it, getting away at 1pm.

On the main line earlier that morning, 4-6-0 No 7006 *Lydford Castle* had taken up the 7.30am from Penzance to Manchester train, closely followed by 4-6-0 No 5075 *Wellington* on an up Ocean Liner special. However, the up 'Torbay Express' was cancelled due to the fog, but its locomotive 4-6-0 No 4090 *Dorchester Castle* arrived in Newton Abbot at 12.12pm with headboard reversed, hauling two non-corridor coaches and two through coaches to be attached to the front of the 7.55am from Penzance to Swansea, hauled by 4-6-0 No 6936 *Breccles Hall*.

Above:

This is the opposing view to that shown earlier on Page 12, taken from a spot alongside the road bridge, showing the south (or west in GWR parlance) end of Newton Abbot station on 25 June 1961, with 2-6-2T No 6146 leaving platform No 2 with the Paignton portion of the 10.10am Sunday Wolverhampton (Low Level) to Penzance train. The main train had been hauled by B-B Type 4 diesel-hydraulic No D834 *Pathfinder*, running almost exactly an hour late, not that this was too unusual for long distance Sunday trains in those days. Only the rear coaches on the Paignton train have come from Wolverhampton. Those

at the front have been drawn out of the well-stocked carriage sidings alongside the station, and will probably provide accommodation for school pupils on Monday morning. Looming large in the background is the Newton Abbot power station, opened in 1924, just three years before the new railway station. This provided coal traffic for the railway, much of which came up from Kingswear, where it was brought in by coastal shipping. The cleared area on the right was occupied by railway cottages until 1940, when these were demolished following a bombing raid on the town, which also hit the station and engine shed yard.

At the near end of the yard is BR Class 9F 2-10-0 No 92233.

Right:

On Saturday 12 August 1961 4-6-0 No 4975 *Umberslade Hall* climbs the 1 in 73 gradient above Torre station with homegoing holidaymakers on the 8.50am from Paignton to Leeds, as 4-6-0 No 5003 *Lulworth Castle* drops down into Torquay with the 8am Exeter to Kingswear local service. *Lulworth Castle* later worked the up 'Torbay Express' from Kingswear to Paddington.

For many years the 216 mile run between Shrewsbury and Newton Abbot had been the longest double-home turn for the men and machines of both depots, hauling the morning Liverpool / Manchester to Penzance / Kingswear train, returning with the corresponding working next day. Even during the war, each shed turned out an immaculate engine, normally a `Castle´, for this working, and the tradition continued to the end of the steam era, when someone decided to obtain a few more miles from the engine by extending its working down to Kingswear. Until then the engine had normally been detached at Newton Abbot and gone on shed. Thus it was that in 1961 there was each evening the spectacle of a gleaming `Castle´ going down to Kingswear, normally with the Kingswear portion of the down `Royal Duchy´ from Paddington, but if the Manchester was running late the two branch portions were combined, as here behind 4-6-0 No 5095 *Barbury Castle* from 84G (Salop) leaving Torquay on Monday 24 April 1961.

The same train is seen again, two months later, on Monday 19 June 1961, with a Shrewsbury 'Castle', and with both portions now strengthened for the summer service, it is a more substantial train of nine or 10 coaches. This time the 'Royal Duchy' coaches are leading, behind 4-6-0 No 5059 *Earl St Aldwyn*, as it climbs high above Goodrington beach on which many people are taking an evening stroll. The Manchester coaches have been joined by a Liverpool portion for the summer months and these were due off Goodrington Sands Halt — seen behind the tail of the train — at 5.34pm. Likewise the London coaches were booked to leave Goodrington at 6.3pm. The time is now 6.40pm. Note the five sidings of Happy Valley, opposite the Halt, full of spare coaches, many of which will not turn a wheel until the following Saturday.

Above:

Later that summer, No 5059 *Earl St Aldwyn* is seen again, this time on Wednesday evening 30 August 1961, after arrival at Kingswear, shunting stock out across Hoodown viaduct, with Waterhead Creek in the background. On this occasion the train from the north had evidently been 'on time', since this portion was worked down to Kingswear independently, with *Earl St Aldwyn* following later on the 'Royal Duchy' coaches. The South Devon Railway had opened the branch as far as Torquay (Torre) in December 1848,

but the Dartmouth & Torbay Railway did not reach Kingswear until 1864. The whole area occupied by Kingswear station and the then quite extensive carriage sidings was on land reclaimed from the River Dart.

Right:

Churston station at 10.34am on 11 March 1960, as 2-6-2T No 5158 leaves for Newton Abbot with the 10.25am from Kingswear to Bristol. At Newton Abbot these coaches will be attached to the 7.30am from

Penzance to Manchester. In the bay platform, an immaculate 0-4-2T No 1470 is ready to return to Brixham with the 11.7am auto working. The estate agents' notices were a permanent feature of the branch waiting shelter, on the side facing the main road, while in the up side bay fish vans await traffic from Brixham. On summer Saturdays the courtyard outside Churston station would be alive with buses and coaches taking holidaymakers to and from the holiday camps south of Brixham, an area remote from the branch terminus.

It is appropriate that we end our tour of Devon at Newton Abbot, in steam days the hub of locomotive operations in the southwest. Newton Abbot was also the place where I made most of my early observations of locomotive and train workings, starting as many people did, while at school in those interesting war years, and continuing on and off to the present time, though latterly far more off than on! On 25 June 1961 we see the approach to Newton Abbot from Kingswear and Plymouth as 4-6-0 No 7037 *Swindon*, the last 'Castle' class engine to be built, nears the station with the 4.5pm (Sunday) from Paignton to Paddington.

Above:

The 27 January 1962 was a red-letter day in the West Country steam calendar, because Plymouth Argyle were at home to Tottenham Hotspur in the third round of the FA Cup, and this was likely to mean steam-hauled excursion trains at a time when most of the regular trains were behind diesel-hydraulics. We were not to be disappointed. Four trains ran. The first at 5.45am from Broxbourne arrived behind 4-6-0 No 5015 *Kingswear Castle*, followed by three excursions from Paddington hauled by 4-6-0s Nos 6009

King Charles II, No 6027 *King Richard I* and 6015 *King Richard III*. In the evening the Paddington excursions returned behind Nos 5015 *Kingswear Castle*, 6027 *King Richard I* and 4095 *Harlech Castle*, while the 6.20pm Plymouth to Broxbourne had No 7022 *Hereford Castle*, piloted into Newton Abbot by No 4087 *Cardigan Castle*. This excursion is depicted at Newton Abbot, while alongside in platform No 7 is 4-6-0 No 4991 *Cobham Hall* on the 7.30pm parcels train to Taunton, to which 2-6-0 No 7311 was later

attached as pilot.

Rear cover:

Seaton Junction station on 28 June 1958. Adams Radial 4-4-2T No 30584, returning from the Lyme Regis branch to Exmouth Junction shed, waits in the down platform, as Class 'M7' 0-4-4T No 30046 leaves on a train to Seaton.

BCA
91 NEWMAN STREET
LONDON
W1.

Membership Number UT23596538

Current Member Purchase
  9638   STEAM IN DEVON   8.50

AMOUNT DUE   8.50

CASH   20.00
CHANGE DUE   11.50

BRANCH   50 02/
RECEIPT 024939 DATE 01 03 96 TIME 13:56

THANK YOU FOR YOUR CUSTOM.